DATE DUE

Demco No. 62-0549

YOUNG TURKEY

Other books in this series

YOUNG FRANCE

YOUNG ISRAEL

YOUNG JAPAN

YOUNG PUERTO RICO

YOUNG RUSSIA

YOUNG SPAIN

Children of Turkey at work and at play

YOUNG
TURKEY

by Marianna Norris

PHOTOGRAPHS BY
ARA GULER

Dodd, Mead & Company · New York

For Laurie, Michelle, Sim and Timur

ACKNOWLEDGMENTS

The author wishes to acknowledge the cooperation of members of Turkey's Ministry of Tourism and Information: Niyazi Babür, Burhan Doğançay, Tahsin Karacabey, Vedia Okan, Akil Serdaroğlu, Memduh Tezel, Ayhan Uytun.

Photographs on pages 5, 22 and 51 are from the Ministry of Tourism and Information. Those on pages 39 (top), 45 and 49, by Nâzim Geray, Mustafa Berkalp and Gülben Süngitay, respectively, are from *Hürriyet*. Those on page 61, by Yurdaer Acar, are from Haber Ajansi.

When you first hear about Turkey, it sounds like a fairy-tale country.

Turkish children walk to school on roads that Marco Polo traveled. They play hide-and-seek in castles built by the Crusaders and do farm chores on the slopes of Mount Ararat where Noah landed the Ark.

For seven hundred years, the country was ruled by Sultans. There were wise and good ones, at first. Afterwards, there were cruel ones who were against any change or progress. It was only forty years ago that Ataturk, the Turkish George Washington, overthrew the last Sultan and proclaimed a Republic. Starting out centuries behind the western countries, Ataturk decreed an end to backward customs and old-fashioned dress. He brought the nation new ideas of liberty and equality, and said there must be education and opportunity even for the poor.

It takes years to remake an entire country and the Turks' gallant struggle is still going on.

The children of Turkey are an important part of that struggle. During the War of Independence, they made bullets, carried supplies to the front and fought beside their parents. Now, in quieter times, they still grow up with a great love of "Vatan," the Fatherland, and a desire to help fulfill Ataturk's ideals.

If you should meet these children, you'd find their names hard to pronounce, at first. Yashar, Ugur, Saban . . . those are boys. A girl may be called Vedia, which means "gift," or Yildiz, which is "star," or Nilufer—"waterlily." The country they live in lies partly on the southeast tip of Europe, partly on the great oblong peninsula of Asia Minor. The peninsula, ringed with rugged mountains, rises to a high, windswept plateau. In its center is the rocky citadel of Ankara, the Turkish capital.

On the northern coast, the mountains drop steeply to the Black Sea, cut by fantastic ravines and thickly forested with cedar and oak. Turkish Girl and Boy Scouts plant thousands more trees here every year.

The mountains are highest and wildest on the eastern border, where the great rivers Tigris and Euphrates rise. On the western coast, the Aegean Sea is filled with a jigsaw puzzle of green islands. Centuries ago, this was a pirate coast but today the hidden bays and slopes are given over to fishing villages and vineyards.

Southern Turkey has a balmy climate all year round. Antalya, with its twenty-seven rivers, is a perfect place for vacationing.

We like to call America a "melting pot" because so many different kinds of people have enriched our culture in the last two hundred years. Turkey is a melting pot, too. But there the melting and enriching have been going on for 10,000 years!

Besides the Turks themselves, who came from Central Asia, there have been Greeks and Romans, Kurds and Circassians, Arabs and Armenians, Persians and Tartars, traveling the route from Europe to Asia and from Asia to Europe. Some of each race stayed to raise their families in the place called Anatolia, Land of the Sunrise.

Because of this rich heritage, Turkey is many kinds of country in one. When you see a child of Istanbul or Ankara or Izmir at work or play, you will say that he is just like an American. Turkish country children, with their odd clothes, will be harder for you to recognize. But when you see them enjoying a bite of candy, worrying about their exams, or hugging their mothers, suddenly you will recognize them and like them.

The old Turkish story-tellers used to tell their audiences, "I will speak of fantastic wonders, of fairies and marvelous animals and giants, and good and evil genies! And I warn you that in all my tale there is not a single word of truth!"

The story of Turkey itself is full of wonders of nature, marvels of history, fabulous animals and giant projects . . . but every word of it is true. Here, to prove it, are pictures of the children whose daily lives are lived in this unique country.

Daisies and red poppies grow wild for the picking in the part of Turkey that is in Europe. Beyond them, flowing placidly, you can see the strait of water called the Bosphorus. The other shore is another continent. A ferry will take you there for ten cents.

When you land, you are in Asia. The first thousand miles of it are Turkish, from the fashionable suburb on the shore to far-off walled cities where little girls walk to market on streets of dirt.

In Europe and Asia alike, Turks have one thing in common—
their love of family life.

You can see it in a big back yard in Istanbul as two little boys
enjoy a walk with their grandfather, the second President of the
Republic.

You can feel its warmth in the courtyard of a village home as
the smell of a good goose dinner calls the family together.

You will find the same family affection on the far borders of Turkey where the restless mountain tribes live. These tribes have roamed the wild eastern highlands for thousands of years, always fiercely independent of their neighbors. In recent years, the Republic has brought good schools to the eastern villages and many of the tribespeople, wanting their children to be educated, are coming down from the mountains to take a part in Turkish life.

A mountain mother wears a mark on her forehead to show which tribe she belongs to. Her family's clothes may look strange to you. But in America, the Pennsylvania Dutch wear clothes very different from their neighbors, and Navajo shepherds still dress as their grandfathers did. Turkey, too, has many communities where people cling to ancient dress.

Young people in up-to-date Istanbul are as surprised at these costumes as you are.

If you had been born in Istanbul, like this baby, you would have grown up just about the way you did.

But around Zonguldak, in northern Turkey, your mother would have carried you in a blanket, close on her back, to protect you from the cold.

A back pack serves for a baby carriage in the south, too, because
mother needs her hands free for work in the fields.

In Yozgat, baby strollers are scarce but a donkey's saddlebag does the same job. Notice the ladies' trousers? They're very practical for farmwork and comfortable for riding, too. The head scarf keeps off sun and dust.

Along with plenty of affection, Turkish children get plenty of discipline. City or country, they learn early that it's important to obey your parents.

Waiting for the school bus, or carrying a bunch of wildflowers to his teacher, you can always tell a Turkish schoolboy by his uniform.

You start school when you're seven in Turkey, going five hours a day. Sometimes, there's a split shift because of the teacher shortage. Then, half the children go in the morning from 8:30 to 12:30 and the others go from 12:50 to 4:50 in the afternoon.

The five years of Primary School are compulsory. After that, many children go on to three years of Middle School and three of High School. Subjects studied are just about the same as in America, except that foreign languages are started earlier. History classes, of course, teach Turkey's exciting past.

In High School, the hours are from 9 till 4, four days a week, and 9 till 12 Wednesday and Saturday. Most schools are co-educational. In the square outside Istanbul's Blue Mosque, you'll often see High School boys and girls studying together in their lunch hour.

The girls have a wide choice of professions open to them. In Turkey, women are taken for granted as chemists, veterinarians, engineers and architects. Girls can even enter the Turkish West Point. Turkey had the first woman fighter pilot and the first woman Supreme Court judge.

Less than fifty years ago, women wore veils in Turkey and some spent their lives in harems. If you asked a man how many children he had, he would tell you only the number of boys.

All that changed after the revolution. Mustafa Kemal Ataturk, who founded the Turkish Republic, made sure that equality for all was written into the Constitution.

Mustafa Kemal Ataturk
1881-1938

Ataturk believed that education was all-important. In his day, only 15 per cent of Turks could read and write. One reason was that their language was written in the Arabic alphabet which has 612 letters and is very difficult to learn. You can see some of it in the old inscription on the wall of this public fountain in Bursa. Ataturk changed the Turkish language over to our alphabet with its 26 easy letters. After that, millions more people were able to learn to read and write.

If you turn the picture upside down, you'll see that the boy is reading the sports page and probably worrying about his team, Fenerbahce. The Turks love soccer. They get as excited about it as we get about baseball. Fenerbahce and Galatasaray are like the Dodgers and the Yankees. Whenever they play, the nation's boys are in a turmoil, rooting for one team or the other.

There's no television in Turkey, so most boys can't watch Fenerbahce play. Instead, they get out and play themselves.

A sport that's peculiarly Turkish is *guresh*—wrestling. Turks keep alive a very ancient style of wrestling for which they wear long leather trousers and oil their bodies to make them slippery.

The championships are held in a grassy field near Edirne on the Greek-Bulgarian border. Boys compete on the first day of the festival. They still perform ancient ceremonies before each match. While they wrestle, a bass drum booms and an oboe wails traditional music.

Turkey has nearly five thousand miles of shoreline, from the fine dark sand beaches of the north that gave the Black Sea its name, to the sun-drenched Turkish Riviera in the south, with its palm trees and castles on the blue Mediterranean.

Swimming is fun and skin diving a real adventure because hundreds of ancient shipwrecks lie in the off-shore waters, waiting to be explored.

The names of the games Turkish children play are different—
Wolf and Lamb . . . Hare, Find Your Home—but you wouldn't be
out of things for long, on a summer evening on Istiklal Street. From
Ring Around the Rosy to Cops and Robbers, they're all the same
games you play at home, once you get past the titles.

Chelik-Chomak means Bat-Stick and it's very much like baseball. Open the Door, Chief Merchant turns out to be exactly like
London Bridge, with a tug-of-war at the end.

Hide-and-Seek, Simon Says, Did You Ever See a Lassie?—all
have their Turkish equivalents.

Turkish children even have their Eeny Meeny Miney Mo. It's a nonsense rhyme beginning *Oh, mo, eeney, battey* . . . . And guess who Cifci Cukurdadir is? Your friend, the Farmer in the Dell.

The Istanbul Amusement Park, closed in winter, is a favorite place for flying kites.

Toys? They're the same everywhere. If you can, you buy them. If you can't, you make them, as this Bursa boy made himself an American car.

"Balloons! Balloons! Fifteen *kurush* for a balloon!"

A *kurush* is a Turkish penny. Lots of young Turks are out earning them to help their families.

80385

Summers are hot in Izmir. It feels good to sit down by
the cool harbor and splash water on your face. After that,
back to work with the big brass jug, selling cold water in
the public square.

Sometimes whole families work together. Hazelnuts are the cash crop in Bolu. (Turkey grows more of them than any other country.) When the harvest is in, everyone in the village pitches in, sorting the nuts and getting them ready for the market.

The herdsman has a lonelier job. Often one boy takes the sheep and goats of the whole village out to pasture. He knows all the animals apart and, in the evening, drops each one off at its own home.

In hot climates or in cold ones, goats are much hardier than cows. While you've been drinking cow's milk all your life, most Turkish children have been drinking goat's milk.

These are Angora goats. (Angora was the old name of Ankara, the capital.) Remember the legend of Jason searching for the Golden Fleece? The kingdom where he found it is a part of Turkey. Today, people still go there to get the longest, silkiest fleece in the world from the Angora goat.

In summer, a shepherd may take his flock high into the mountains and stay for months, bringing it down only when the weather gets too cold.

Farming is Turkey's biggest business—growing wheat, cotton, tobacco, sugar beets, grapes, figs, olives, rice and tea. The big farms have tractors and modern machines to do the work but on the small farms there are plenty of chores for the son of the family.

Country daughters have their duties, too. One of them is spinning wool. Another is knitting warm socks.

One of Turkey's ancient arts is weaving carpets.

Twist . . . knot . . . tighten . . .

Clip the dark blue, the cream, the red . . .

The pattern that appears has been passed down from mother to daughter for five centuries!

Water from a faucet is an unknown luxury in many Turkish villages. You get water from a spring or from a public fountain in the square. Usually, it is the girls' job to fetch it, morning and evening. It looks like hard work, but country children are strong and husky.

In the city, of course, a little Turkish girl has modern conveniences to make her chores easier.

Coastal Turks are famous for their sailor skills and their children are busy helpers in the fishing fleet.

Sometimes the boys ride high on the mast, spotting for dolphins or schools of fish. The girls help mend sails and nets and bring provisions down to the boats.

Both girls and boys spend hours on the beach, gathering mussels and edible seaweed for the family.

When it comes to cooking, the Turks are masters. They make *shish kebab* (lamb cooked on a skewer over an open flame), *dolma* (vine leaves stuffed with rice and black currants and pine nuts), *börek* (pastry with salted cheese or ground lamb inside).

Turks prepare vegetables in all kinds of surprising and tasty ways. Usually, they cook them long before the meal because they prefer to eat them cold. One concoction of eggplant and olive oil is so rich that it's called *Imam Bayildi* . . . "The Preacher Fainted." A roast meat dish is called "His Majesty Liked It." And for dessert you can choose between "Twisted Turban" and "Vizier's Fingers."

Turkish fruits are famous. Oranges, bananas and pomegranates come from the south, strawberries from the northern provinces, peaches from Bursa and honeylip figs from Izmir.

Black cherries were first introduced to the West by Roman soldiers stationed on the Black Sea. In fact, our word "cherries" comes from the name of the Turkish town where they were found in such abundance — Giresun.

Around Diyarbakir, on the banks of the Euphrates River, melons are the farmers' pride. They grow some so small you can pickle them whole, others so big that a camel can only carry one on each side.

Out in the country, the farm people bake brown bread in round loaves. With it, they eat black olives and onions and white cheese made from goat's milk or yogurt made from sheep's milk.

Turks, young and old, have a sweet tooth. Honey, ground almonds, sesame are all made into different kinds of candy. Perhaps you've tasted their *halvah* in this country. Their *lokum* is famous everywhere as "Turkish Delight." Sugar apples are a favorite with children.

Little boys who do their chores well often get *majoon* as a reward. *Majoon* is a thick, jellied candy on a stick. The men who sell it play the clarinet as they come down the street. You know how American children run when they hear the bells of the ice cream wagon coming? Turkish children run that way toward the sound of the *majoon* vendor's clarinet.

A hundred years before our Society for the Prevention of Cruelty to Animals was founded, a European traveler reported that he couldn't even beat his horse in the streets of Turkey without a lot of Turks running out to stop him.

Turks love animals!

Even wild animals are made into pets and you'll often find a gypsy playing the tambourine while a big brown bear dances.

Pigeons, they say, are Allah's messengers. Storks are supposed to bring good luck. One of the birds' favorite meeting places is in front of Istanbul's Eyub Mosque. With their flapping and their cooing, they fill the plaza with a lovely soothing racket, all day long.

Most Turks are Moslems—followers of Mohammed. Their churches are mosques, domed outside and brightly tiled inside. The one above is tiled in a hundred shades of blue.

51

You leave your shoes at the door and wear slippers when you go into a mosque. The sacred book of the Moslems is the Koran. Reading it, memorizing parts, and living according to its high ideals are the main points in a Moslem religious education.

At twelve years, a Moslem boy has a coming-of-age celebration with gifts and feasting. It starts with a visit to a mosque. This boy comes to Eyub Mosque because Eyub was a great hero of the faith and his mosque is the most sacred place in Istanbul.

Behind the Eyub Mosque, boys drive their sheep past grave-stones of the Turks who, back in 1453, conquered the great Byzantine city of Constantinople and made it Istanbul.

You can never forget history in Turkey. It rises up all around you. Two thousand years ago, Asia Minor was a Roman province. Antony and Cleopatra met in the town of Tarsus. At Zile, Julius Caesar defeated the Persians and said, "I came, I saw, I conquered!"

There are toppled Roman cities everywhere. All over Turkey, you can still walk on Roman roads or, if you are a boy, strike echoes with a handball on a Roman wall.

Long before the Romans, the Greeks built marble cities in Asia
Minor. Earthquakes destroyed most of the palaces and temples,
but tourists still come to see them and Turkish children, who know
the ruins better than anyone, love to be guides. When they are not
showing people around, they are looking for treasure—statues,
Greek pottery and beautiful ancient coins that wash out of the
ground whenever it rains.

Before the Greeks—before history began—there were other civ-
ilizations on Turkish soil. The language, the laws of the Hittites
are a mystery to us. But, carved on stone, they left pictures of their
families. A little girl with a toy. A boy playing with his pet. Suddenly, you see that young Hittites, young Turks, young Americans
are quite a lot alike!

You can see that Turkish children come in all shapes and sizes
. . . in blonde as well as brunette. They come in scholar's caps . . .

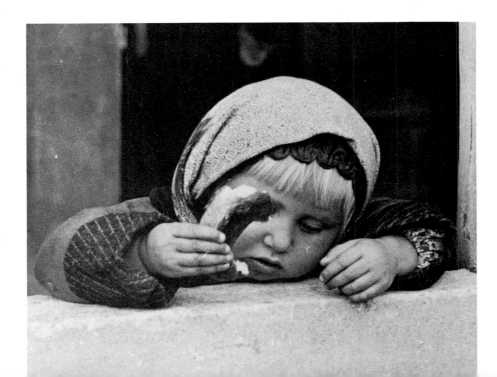

. . . and in the little round hats
worn at coming-of-age parties.

As in America, they come rich and poor. And, as everywhere, the big thing they have in common is that the country's future depends on them. That's why two of the biggest national holidays are Youth Day on May 19 and Children's Day on April 23.

On Children's Day, Turkish children get a preview of grownup responsibilities. They are invited to take charge (with a little supervision!) of the most important government and business offices. They act as judges in the courts and they edit and print the biggest Turkish newspaper, whose name, *Hürriyet*, means Independence.

Out in the streets, red Turkish flags fly. Children parade in national costume and sing the ancient folk songs from each region of Turkey. They do the dagger dances of the East and the wild eagle dance of the Aegean Coast. You can see dancers from Central Turkey snapping fingers and clicking painted wooden spoons like castanets. The Black Sea fisherboys do a tense, leaping dance that reminds you of the ocean. The Mehters are marching—military bands dressed as in the days of the Sultans, with drums and cymbals crashing.

On April 23, it's especially exciting to be a child and to be Turkish.

In a country as new to modern ways as Turkey, children growing up have many problems ahead of them. Most of the things that George Washington fought for have been won, in the last two hundred years. But many of the things Ataturk wanted still need fighting for.

These children will have the job of pushing the frontiers of education and democracy back to their country's far borders. It's a challenge but, when you know the young people of Turkey, you are sure they will be able to meet it!